My Notes

"All I Want to Do is Stay in My PJs, Eat Cookies, Drink Green Tea & Watch Movies All Day Long."

My Notes

"All I Wanna Do is Stay in My PJs, Eat Cookies, Drink Green Tea & Watch Movies All Day Long."

My Notes

"All I Wanna Do is Stay in My PJs, Eat Cookies, Drink Green Tea & Watch Movies All Day Long."

My Notes

"All I Wanna Do is Stay in My Pjs, Eat Cookies, Drink Green Tea & Watch Movies All Day Long."

My Notes

"All I Wanna Do is Stay in My Pjs, Eat Cookies, Drink Green Tea & Watch Movies All Day Long."

My Notes

"All I Wanna Do is Stay in My Pjs, Eat Cookies, Drink Green Tea & Watch Movies All Day Long."

My Notes

"All I Wanna Do is Stay in My Pjs, Eat Cookies, Drink Green Tea & Watch Movies All Day Long."

My Notes

"All I wanna Do is Stay in My PJs, Eat Cookies, Drink Green Tea & Watch Movies All Day Long."

My Notes

"All I Wanna Do is Stay in My Pjs, Eat Cookies, Drink Green Tea & Watch Movies All Day Long."

My Notes

"All I Wanna Do is Stay in My Pjs, Eat Cookies, Drink Green Tea & Watch Movies All Day Long."

My Notes

"All I Wanna Do is Stay in My Pjs, Eat Cookies, Drink Green Tea & Watch Movies All Day Long."

My Notes

"All I Wanna Do is Stay in My Pjs, Eat Cookies, Drink Green Tea & Watch Movies All Day Long."

My Notes

"All I Wanna Do is Stay in My PJs, Eat Cookies, Drink Green Tea & Watch Movies All Day Long."

My Notes

"All I Wanna Do is Stay in My Pjs, Eat Cookies, Drink Green Tea & Watch Movies All Day Long."

My Notes

"All I Wanna Do is Stay in My Pjs, Eat Cookies, Drink Green Tea & Watch Movies All Day Long."

My Notes

"All I Wanna Do is Stay in My Pjs, Eat Cookies, Drink Green Tea & Watch Movies All Day Long."

My Notes

"All I Wanna Do is Stay in My Pjs, Eat Cookies, Drink Green Tea & Watch Movies All Day Long."

My Notes

"All I Wanna Do is Stay in My Pjs, Eat Cookies, Drink Green Tea & Watch Movies All Day Long."

My Notes

"All I Wanna Do is Stay in My Pjs, Eat Cookies, Drink Green Tea & Watch Movies All Day Long."

My Notes

"All I Wanna Do is Stay in My Pjs, Eat Cookies, Drink Green Tea & Watch Movies All Day Long."

My Notes

"All I Wanna Do is Stay in My Pjs, Eat Cookies, Drink Green Tea & Watch Movies All Day Long."

My Notes

"All I Wanna Do is Stay in My PJs, Eat Cookies, Drink Green Tea & Watch Movies All Day Long."

My Notes

"All I Wanna Do is Stay in My Pjs, Eat Cookies, Drink Green Tea & Watch Movies All Day Long."

My Notes

"All I Wanna Do is Stay in My Pjs, Eat Cookies, Drink Green Tea & Watch Movies All Day Long."

My Notes

"All I Wanna Do is Stay in My Pjs, Eat Cookies, Drink Green Tea & Watch Movies All Day Long."

My Notes

"All I Wanna Do is Stay in My PJs, Eat Cookies, Drink Green Tea & Watch Movies All Day Long."

My Notes

"All I Wanna Do is Stay in My Pjs, Eat Cookies, Drink Green Tea & Watch Movies All Day Long."

My Notes

"All I Wanna Do is Stay in My Pjs, Eat Cookies, Drink Green Tea & Watch Movies All Day Long."

My Notes

"All I Wanna Do is Stay in My PJs, Eat Cookies, Drink Green Tea & Watch Movies All Day Long."

My Notes

"All I Wanna Do is Stay in My Pjs, Eat Cookies, Drink Green Tea & Watch Movies All Day Long."

My Notes

"All I Wanna Do is Stay in My Pjs, Eat Cookies, Drink Green Tea & Watch Movies All Day Long."

My Notes

"All I Wanna Do is Stay in My Pjs, Eat Cookies, Drink Green Tea & Watch Movies All Day Long."

My Notes

"All I Wanna Do is Stay in My Pjs, Eat Cookies, Drink Green Tea & Watch Movies All Day Long."

My Notes

"All I Wanna Do is Stay in My PJs, Eat Cookies, Drink Green Tea & Watch Movies All Day Long."

My Notes

"All I Wanna Do is Stay in My PJs, Eat Cookies, Drink Green Tea & Watch Movies All Day Long."

My Notes

"All I Wanna Do is Stay in My Pjs, Eat Cookies, Drink Green Tea & Watch Movies All Day Long."

My Notes

"All I Wanna Do is Stay in My Pjs, Eat Cookies, Drink Green Tea & Watch Movies All Day Long."

My Notes

"All I Wanna Do is Stay in My Pjs, Eat Cookies, Drink Green Tea & Watch Movies All Day Long."

My Notes

"All I Wanna Do is Stay in My Pjs, Eat Cookies, Drink Green Tea & Watch Movies All Day Long."

My Notes

"All I Wanna Do is Stay in My Pjs, Eat Cookies, Drink Green Tea & Watch Movies All Day Long."

My Notes

"All I Wanna Do is Stay in My Pjs, Eat Cookies, Drink Green Tea & Watch Movies All Day Long."

My Notes

"All I Wanna Do is Stay in My Pjs, Eat Cookies, Drink Green Tea & Watch Movies All Day Long."

My Notes

"All I Wanna Do is Stay in My Pjs, Eat Cookies, Drink Green Tea & Watch Movies All Day Long."

My Notes

"All I Wanna Do is Stay in My Pjs, Eat Cookies, Drink Green Tea & Watch Movies All Day Long."

My Notes

"All I Wanna Do is Stay in My Pjs, Eat Cookies, Drink Green Tea & Watch Movies All Day Long."

My Notes

"All I Wanna Do is Stay in My Pjs, Eat Cookies, Drink Green Tea & Watch Movies All Day Long."

My Notes

"All I Wanna Do is Stay in My Pjs, Eat Cookies, Drink Green Tea & Watch Movies All Day Long."

My Notes

"All I wanna Do is Stay in My Pjs, Eat Cookies, Drink Green Tea & Watch Movies All Day Long."

My Notes

"All I Wanna Do is Stay in My Pjs, Eat Cookies, Drink Green Tea & Watch Movies All Day Long."

My Notes

"All I Wanna Do is Stay in My Pjs, Eat Cookies, Drink Green Tea & Watch Movies All Day Long."

My Notes

"All I Wanna Do is Stay in My Pjs, Eat Cookies, Drink Green Tea & Watch Movies All Day Long."

My Notes

"All I Wanna Do is Stay in My PJs, Eat Cookies, Drink Green Tea & Watch Movies All Day Long."

My Notes

"All I Wanna Do is Stay in My Pjs, Eat Cookies, Drink Green Tea & Watch Movies All Day Long."

My Notes

"All I Wanna Do is Stay in My Pjs, Eat Cookies, Drink Green Tea & Watch Movies All Day Long."

My Notes

"All I Wanna Do is Stay in My Pjs, Eat Cookies, Drink Green Tea & Watch Movies All Day Long."

My Notes

"All I Wanna Do is Stay in My Pjs, Eat Cookies, Drink Green Tea & Watch Movies All Day Long."

My Notes

"All I Wanna Do is Stay in My Pjs, Eat Cookies, Drink Green Tea & Watch Movies All Day Long."

My Notes

"All I Wanna Do is Stay in My PJs, Eat Cookies, Drink Green Tea & Watch Movies All Day Long."

My Notes

"All I Wanna Do is Stay in My Pjs, Eat Cookies, Drink Green Tea & Watch Movies All Day Long."

My Notes

"All I Wanna Do is Stay in My PJs, Eat Cookies, Drink Green Tea & Watch Movies All Day Long."

My Notes

"All I Wanna Do is Stay in My Pjs, Eat Cookies, Drink Green Tea & Watch Movies All Day Long."

My Notes

"All I Wanna Do is Stay in My PJs, Eat Cookies, Drink Green Tea & Watch Movies All Day Long."

My Notes

"All I Wanna Do is Stay in My Pjs, Eat Cookies, Drink Green Tea & Watch Movies All Day Long."

My Notes

"All I Wanna Do is Stay in My Pjs, Eat Cookies, Drink Green Tea & Watch Movies All Day Long."

My Notes

"All I Wanna Do is Stay in My Pjs, Eat Cookies, Drink Green Tea & Watch Movies All Day Long."

My Notes

"All I Wanna Do is Stay in My Pjs, Eat Cookies, Drink Green Tea & Watch Movies All Day Long."

My Notes

"All I Wanna Do is Stay in My Pjs, Eat Cookies, Drink Green Tea & Watch Movies All Day Long."

My Notes

"All I Wanna Do is Stay in My Pjs, Eat Cookies, Drink Green Tea & Watch Movies All Day Long."

My Notes

"All I Wanna Do is Stay in My Pjs, Eat Cookies, Drink Green Tea & Watch Movies All Day Long."

My Notes

"All I Wanna Do is Stay in My PJs, Eat Cookies, Drink Green Tea & Watch Movies All Day Long."

My Notes

"All I Wanna Do is Stay in My Pjs, Eat Cookies, Drink Green Tea & Watch Movies All Day Long."

My Notes

"All I Wanna Do is Stay in My Pjs, Eat Cookies, Drink Green Tea & Watch Movies All Day Long."

My Notes

"All I Wanna Do is Stay in My Pjs, Eat Cookies, Drink Green Tea & Watch Movies All Day Long."

My Notes

"All I Wanna Do is Stay in My Pjs, Eat Cookies, Drink Green Tea & Watch Movies All Day Long."

My Notes

"All I Wanna Do is Stay in My Pjs, Eat Cookies, Drink Green Tea & Watch Movies All Day Long."

My Notes

"All I Wanna Do is Stay in My PJs, Eat Cookies, Drink Green Tea & Watch Movies All Day Long."

My Notes

"All I Wanna Do is Stay in My PJs, Eat Cookies, Drink Green Tea & Watch Movies All Day Long."

My Notes

"All I Wanna Do is Stay in My Pjs, Eat Cookies, Drink Green Tea & Watch Movies All Day Long."

My Notes

"All I Wanna Do is Stay in My Pjs, Eat Cookies, Drink Green Tea & Watch Movies All Day Long."

My Notes

"All I Wanna Do is Stay in My PJs, Eat Cookies, Drink Green Tea & Watch Movies All Day Long."

My Notes

"All I Wanna Do is Stay in My Pjs, Eat Cookies, Drink Green Tea & Watch Movies All Day Long."

My Notes

"All I Wanna Do is Stay in My Pjs, Eat Cookies, Drink Green Tea & Watch Movies All Day Long."

My Notes

"All I Wanna Do is Stay in My PJs, Eat Cookies, Drink Green Tea & Watch Movies All Day Long."

My Notes

"All I Wanna Do is Stay in My Pjs, Eat Cookies, Drink Green Tea & Watch Movies All Day Long."

My Notes

"All I Wanna Do is Stay in My Pjs, Eat Cookies, Drink Green Tea & Watch Movies All Day Long."

My Notes

"All I Wanna Do is Stay in My PJs, Eat Cookies, Drink Green Tea & Watch Movies All Day Long."

My Notes

"All I Wanna Do is Stay in My Pjs, Eat Cookies, Drink Green Tea & Watch Movies All Day Long."

My Notes

"All I Wanna Do is Stay in My Pjs, Eat Cookies, Drink Green Tea & Watch Movies All Day Long."

My Notes

"All I Wanna Do is Stay in My Pjs, Eat Cookies, Drink Green Tea & Watch Movies All Day Long."

My Notes

"All I Wanna Do is Stay in My Pjs, Eat Cookies, Drink Green Tea & Watch Movies All Day Long."

My Notes

"All I Wanna Do is Stay in My PJs, Eat Cookies, Drink Green Tea & Watch Movies All Day Long."

My Notes

"All I Wanna Do is Stay in My PJs, Eat Cookies, Drink Green Tea & Watch Movies All Day Long."

My Notes

"All I Wanna Do is Stay in My Pjs, Eat Cookies, Drink Green Tea & Watch Movies All Day Long."

My Notes

"All I Wanna Do is Stay in My Pjs, Eat Cookies, Drink Green Tea & Watch Movies All Day Long."

My Notes

"All I Wanna Do is Stay in My Pjs, Eat Cookies, Drink Green Tea & Watch Movies All Day Long."

My Notes

"All I Wanna Do is Stay in My Pjs, Eat Cookies, Drink Green Tea & Watch Movies All Day Long."

My Notes

"All I Wanna Do is Stay in My Pjs, Eat Cookies, Drink Green Tea & Watch Movies All Day Long."

My Notes

"All I Wanna Do is Stay in My Pjs, Eat Cookies, Drink Green Tea & Watch Movies All Day Long."

My Notes

"All I Wanna Do is Stay in My Pjs, Eat Cookies, Drink Green Tea & Watch Movies All Day Long."

My Notes

"All I Wanna Do is Stay in My Pjs, Eat Cookies, Drink Green Tea & Watch Movies All Day Long."

My Notes

"All I Wanna Do is Stay in My Pjs, Eat Cookies, Drink Green Tea & Watch Movies All Day Long."

My Notes

"All I Wanna Do is Stay in My Pjs, Eat Cookies, Drink Green Tea & Watch Movies All Day Long."

My Notes

"All I Wanna Do is Stay in My Pjs, Eat Cookies, Drink Green Tea & Watch Movies All Day Long."

My Notes

"All I Wanna Do is Stay in My PJs, Eat Cookies, Drink Green Tea & Watch Movies All Day Long."

My Notes

"All I Wanna Do is Stay in My Pjs, Eat Cookies, Drink Green Tea & Watch Movies All Day Long."

My Notes

"All I Wanna Do is Stay in My PJs, Eat Cookies, Drink Green Tea & Watch Movies All Day Long."

My Notes

"All I Wanna Do is Stay in My Pjs, Eat Cookies, Drink Green Tea & Watch Movies All Day Long."

My Notes

"All I Wanna Do is Stay in My Pjs, Eat Cookies, Drink Green Tea & Watch Movies All Day Long."

My Notes

"All I Wanna Do is Stay in My PJs, Eat Cookies, Drink Green Tea & Watch Movies All Day Long."

My Notes

"All I Wanna Do is Stay in My Pjs, Eat Cookies, Drink Green Tea & Watch Movies All Day Long."

My Notes

"All I Wanna Do is Stay in My Pjs, Eat Cookies, Drink Green Tea & Watch Movies All Day Long."

My Notes

"All I Wanna Do is Stay in My PJs, Eat Cookies, Drink Green Tea & Watch Movies All Day Long."

My Notes

"All I Wanna Do is Stay in My Pjs, Eat Cookies, Drink Green Tea & Watch Movies All Day Long."

My Notes

"All I Wanna Do is Stay in My Pjs, Eat Cookies, Drink Green Tea & Watch Movies All Day Long."

My Notes

"All I Wanna Do is Stay in My PJs, Eat Cookies, Drink Green Tea & Watch Movies All Day Long."

My Notes

"All I Wanna Do is Stay in My PJs, Eat Cookies, Drink Green Tea & Watch Movies All Day Long."

My Notes

"All I Wanna Do is Stay in My PJs, Eat Cookies, Drink Green Tea & Watch Movies All Day Long."

My Notes

"All I Wanna Do is Stay in My PJs, Eat Cookies, Drink Green Tea & Watch Movies All Day Long."

My Notes

"All I Wanna Do is Stay in My Pjs, Eat Cookies, Drink Green Tea & Watch Movies All Day Long."

My Notes

"All I Wanna Do is Stay in My Pjs, Eat Cookies, Drink Green Tea & Watch Movies All Day Long."

www.ingramcontent.com/pod-product-compliance
Ingram Content Group UK Ltd.
Pitfield, Milton Keynes, MK11 3LW, UK
UKHW022240230426
12048UKWH00018BA/1373